Great Scientists: Detectives at Work

by Ronda Greenberg

Scott Foresman
is an imprint of

Glenview, Illinois • Boston, Massachusetts • Chandler, Arizona
Upper Saddle River, New Jersey

ISBN 13: 978-0-328-50797-9
ISBN 10:   0-328-50797-0

What does a detective do?

A detective looks at mysteries and then figures out what happened. Sometimes a detective predicts, or guesses about, what might happen next.

How do detectives solve mysteries? They search for an **explanation** for things that happened. They look for clues, ask a lot of questions, and pay close attention to the answers.

This police officer asks a girl about something she saw on her way home from school.

Who can be a detective?

Some detectives are police officers. They solve crimes. They find out who broke the law. They also help find missing and stolen things.

Some detectives are private **investigators.** People hire them to find out where something or someone might be.

There is also another person who is a kind of detective. That person is a scientist.

Just like a detective, a scientist often figures out what has happened, why it happened, and what might happen next.

This person is a scientist. She is asking herself questions about what happened to the liquid in the test tube.

Detectives often start with one big question, such as *What happened?* or *What caused the accident?*

Scientists also have big questions, such as *How does your brain work?* or *What will tomorrow's weather be like?*

Just like detectives, scientists must look for clues that will help them find the answers to their questions. They study the clues to find facts—information that is known to be true.

This scientist studies dinosaurs. He has a big question: Where did dinosaurs live?

He is looking for clues that will help him answer the question. He has found a **fossil** of an animal footprint. It looks like this track could have belonged to a dinosaur. This fossil is a clue that tells the scientist that dinosaurs might have once lived where the fossil was found.

Scientists look for facts that help answer their questions.

7

What do scientists study?

Both scientists and detectives use their five senses when they are looking for clues. The five senses are seeing, hearing, tasting, touching, and smelling.

In the picture above, the scientist is in the woods. He wants to find out about the weather long ago. He will use one of his senses to find the answer. Which sense do you think he will use?

There are many ways to find out what the weather was like. One way is to look for clues in the trunk of a tree. That is what this scientist is doing.

See the rings on the tree **stump?** Trees grow a new ring every year. So the rings on a tree can tell how old a tree is. They can also tell how much it rained in the place where the tree lives.

If the ring is big, it means there was a lot of rain that year, and the tree grew a lot. If the ring is thin, it means there was not a lot of rain that year, and it didn't grow very much.

Look at the rings. Can you answer the **riddle** of how the weather changed from year to year? Which of the five senses did you use to find the answer?

This photo shows the rings of a tree.

There are many other ways that scientists use their senses to answer questions.

If they **wonder** what a liquid is, they might sniff it to see what it smells like.

This scientist can tell that the liquid in the jar smells sour.

Some scientists are interested in stones. They might feel a stone to find out what kind of stone it is.

Sandstone is soft enough to scratch with your fingernail.

Some scientists work with food. For example, scientists can make flavors for gum or candy. They taste the flavors to see if they are good.

This scientist is trying to make banana bubble gum.

Other scientists work with animals. Listening to the sounds the animals make can help the scientist know how an animal is feeling.

This bird is singing a happy song.

There are many kinds of scientists, but they all use their senses. Have you ever done any science experiments? What senses did you use?

How do scientists and detectives record information?

Both scientists and detectives must remember what they've learned and what questions they need to ask. They use tools to **record** the information.

Look at these pictures. These are some tools that scientists and detectives use. Do you ever use any of these tools to record information?

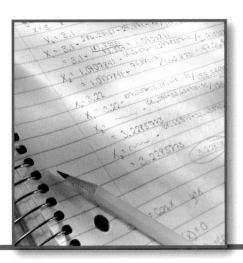

A notebook is very handy. You can write in it or draw pictures wherever you are.

A computer is a very good place to organize information that you have found.

A tape recorder is good for recording what people say when you ask them a question. You can also talk into it yourself to record information and ideas.

With a camera you can take pictures of what you are seeing. Then you can examine the pictures later or use them to show others what you have found.

Scientists and detectives have different kinds of mysteries to solve. But they both work very hard to find the answers to their questions. And these answers will often help a lot of people.

Do you think that being a detective or a scientist sounds like something you would like to do?

Now Try This

In this book, you learned that scientists, like detectives, use their five senses to solve mysteries. Now you will get to use your own senses to solve the mystery of what is in a bag. You will play this game with a partner.

You and your partner will take turns making a mystery bag and guessing what is in it. It is important that you do not peek while your partner is putting the mystery items in the bag.

You will need:

- A brown paper bag.
- Two or three mystery items to put in the bag. These can include pieces of fruit, nuts in or out of their shell, vegetables, coins, or erasers.

Close your bag with tape.
Give the bag to your partner.
This is what your partner should do.

1. Shake the bag to hear how many items are in the bag and what kind of noise they make.
2. Smell the bag.
3. Feel the bag for the shape of the items.
4. Open the bag (BUT DO NOT LOOK INSIDE) and feel the items inside the bag.
5. Guess what the items are.
6. Open the bag, look inside, and see if the guess is correct.
7. Now it is your partner's turn to make a new mystery bag, and it is your turn to be a scientist and use your senses to solve the mystery of what is in the bag.

15

Glossary

explanation *n.* a reason for something

fossil *n.* the remains or tracks of an animal from millions of years ago. A fossil takes the form of a rock

investigators *n.* people who find out about things

record *v.* to keep information

riddle *n.* a question that might seem to make no sense, but has a clever answer

stump *n.* the part of the tree trunk that is left when the tree is cut down

wonder *v.* to want to learn more about something